Digital and Software Piracy

A Selective Annotated Bibliography of Dissertations and Theses

Zander Angelini

Angelini, Zander

Digital and software piracy: A selective annotated bibliography of dissertations and theses/Zander Angelini

p. cm.

1. Computer crimes -- Criticism and Interpretation. 2. Privacy, Right of. I. Title.

HV 6773.2
364.1

ISBN-10   1512297925

ISBN-13   978-1512297928

Cover – Pirate Flag of Captain Jack Rackham, "Calico Jack," 1682-1720

Table of Contents

Digital and Software Piracy

*A Selective Annotated Bibliography of
Dissertations and Theses*

1.)   **Aleassa, H.**

Investigating consumers' software piracy using an extended theory of reasoned action. Ph.D. dissertation, Southern Illinois University at Carbondale. 2009.

Software piracy, the illegal and unauthorized duplication, sale, or distribution of software, is a widespread and costly phenomenon. According to the Business Software Alliance, more than one third of the PC software packages installed worldwide in 2006 were unauthorized copies. This behavior costs the software industry billions of lost dollars in revenue annually. Software piracy behavior has been investigated for more than thirty years. However, there are two voids in the literature: lack of studies in Non-Western countries and scarcity of process studies. As such, this study contributes to the literature by developing a software piracy model to understand the decision making process that underlies this illegal behavior among Jordanian university students. Based on a literature review in various disciplines, including social psychology, psychology, and criminology, several important variables have been incorporated into the proposed model. The model was tested using data collected from a sample of 323 undergraduate business students. The resulting data was analyzed by two main statistical techniques, structural equation modeling (SEM) and hierarchical multiple regression. The results indicated that the model was useful in predicting students' intention to pirate software. Seven out of eight hypotheses were supported. Consistent with The Theory of Reasoned Action, attitudes toward software piracy and subjective norms were significant predictors of intention to pirate software. However, our findings are inconsistent with previous studies with regard to the relative importance of attitude and subjective norms;

subjective norms had a stronger effect. Also, the results suggested that ethical ideology, public self-consciousness, and low self-control moderated the effect of these variables on intention to pirate software. Lastly, the results indicated that the effect of subjective norms on afintention to pirate software was both direct and indirect through attitudes. The results have important practical implications for the software industry and governments to curtail software piracy. Limitations of the study and recommendations for future studies are discussed as well. [Author Abstract]

2.)   **Al-Rafee, S. A.**

Digital piracy: Ethical decision-making.

Ph.D. dissertation, University of Arkansas.

2002.

Software piracy issues have received much interest in the literature (with an estimated $12 billion in lost revenues in 1998 according to the Software Publishers Association). Other forms of piracy have been emerging, such as video and music piracy. Referred to as digital piracy, it is defined as: "The illegal copying and/or downloading of copyrighted software, music, video, or other material (such as MP3s, Hollywood movies, and digital audio books among others)." According to industry estimates (Recording Industry Association of America, Motion Picture Association of America, and the Business Software Alliance), digital piracy caused losses of about $20 billion last year alone. In this research study, a model is developed that would help better explain and understand digital piracy. Using the Theory of Planned Behavior (TPB) as a basis, we extend existing IT ethical behavior models with additional factors based on ethical behavioral literature to further explain digital piracy. A questionnaire was developed and administered to a sample of 292 students. Results of statistical analyses provided general support for the research model (10 out of 13 hypotheses were supported). In summary, digital piracy can be explained by personal attributes and feelings, importance of the issue, attitude, subjective norms, perceived behavioral control, and moral obligation. The results of the study, as well as limitations, implications, and future research are discussed in this presentation. [Author Abstract]

3.)   **Basamanowicz, J. R.**

Release groups and digital copyright piracy.
M.A. thesis, Simon Fraser University
(Canada). 2011.

This study uses data gathered from three US Federal policing operations occurring between 2001 and 2005 that targeted release groups - organized file-sharing groups that obtain commercial content, remove the copyright protection features, and distribute it - and their illicit networks. This data was used to construct a crime-script of these groups' modus operandi to discover methods of disrupting their criminal activities. The results indicate that Industry may increase the risk of releasing content through amendments in DRM, and law enforcement may increase the effort through targeting crackers in prominent release groups. As well, data from a sub-operation of Site Down known as Operation Copy Cat was examined to re-construct a 2-mode network of actors and servers that aimed to distribute copyrighted content. The results of this analysis reveal that although only three individuals received a term of imprisonment, there were as many as five other actors in the network with comparable network centrality that evaded this harsh sentence. [Author Abstract]

4.)   **Behel, J. D.**

An investigation of equity as a determinant of software piracy behavior.

Ph.D. dissertation, University of Arkansas. 1998.

The realization of the computer age has resulted in the rapid proliferation of software and hardware components in both organizations and homes. Today, the total sales is estimated to approach $100 billion a year with another $10 to $12 billion being lost around the world to the illegal copying of software, commonly referred to as software piracy. Though some research has been conducted to better explain the behavior of software piracy, one of the primary determinants of social behavior, equity theory, has not been studied in this context. It is theorized that equity theory is an explanatory factor of the behavior and can be operationalized in an empirical study. The purpose of this study is to identify the components of the latent variable equity in the software piracy context and to evaluate the degree to which equity influences software piracy behavior. A study of literature is used to apply the classical equity dimensions to the equity construct in the software piracy context. An empirical study is used to test and refine the construct. A structural model involving the refined construct and a software piracy construct is then analyzed using a second empirical sample. The analysis is conducted using structural equation modeling. The results in the study are mixed but generally supportive of the proposed model. A refined equity construct is validated. This construct explains a significant portion of the variation in the self-reported software piracy behavior. These findings suggest that the equity construct should be included in any model that attempts to better explain software piracy behavior. The refined equity construct as reflected by the survey items identified in this study is a reliable way to measure the construct. [Author Abstract]

5.) **Butt, A.**

Comparative analysis of software piracy determinants among Pakistani and Canadian university students: Demographics, ethical attitudes and socio-economic factors.
M.Sc. thesis, Simon Fraser University (Canada). 2006.

Software piracy is widespread in many parts of the world. P2P websites such as Kazaa have made it easier to access pirated software, which has resulted in increased emphasis on the issue of software piracy in both the software industry and research community. Some factors that determine piracy include poverty, cultural values, ethical attitudes, religion, and education. Empirical studies have looked at software piracy as an intentional behaviour. This study explores the demographic, ethical and socio-economical factors that can represent software piracy as an unintentional behaviour among a developing country's university students. The author has conducted a comparative analysis of university students from Pakistan and Canada, two countries that differ economically and culturally. The results of the study indicate that software piracy behaviour is different in both groups of students, but that there are also some similarities. Future research directions and implications are also presented. [Author Abstract]

6.)   **Choi, E.**

Investigating factors influencing game piracy in the eSports settings of South Korea.
Ph.D. dissertation, The University of New Mexico. 2013.

eSports, an abbreviation of electronic sports, is a virtual leisure activity (KeSPA, 2011). eSports has been developed through online networks and game software development (Jonasson & Thiborg, 2010), and has commanded national attention and popularity in South Korea. Within cyberspace linked over the Internet or Local Area Networks (LAN's), many participants match electronic game skills against other participants with little spatiotemporal restraint. However, illegal downloading of game materials over the Internet has been prevalent and caused economic losses to game development companies (Korea Creative Content Agency, 2006b). The main purpose of this study was to propose a theoretical model describing determinants of game piracy among eSports game users in South Korea. The study specifically investigated the piracy behaviors of game users according to their demographic background, awareness of copyright laws, and intention to commit game piracy. Using the theory of reasoned action (TRA), the intention was also examined according to attitude towards game piracy and subjective norm. A convenience sample was made up of 354 eSports game users who attended an eSports arena to see the regular season games of a professional league. A binary logistic regression and multiple linear regression analysis were employed to answer the research questions of the study. The results showed that males were more likely to pirate game materials over the Internet than were females. The more intention individuals had, the more they were likely to commit game piracy. Attitude towards game piracy and subjective norm played significant roles in the behavioral intention. Most importantly, the behavioral intention was shaped more by their attitudes towards game piracy than by subjective norms. This study may initially offer people in eSports and game industries, related research communities, and Korean game content agencies an understanding of how and why eSports consumers pirate game materials. By doing so, the findings of the study may inspire further investigation of game-related piracy and policies aimed at reducing the piracy of game content. [Author Abstract]

7.)   **Cohen, M. A.**

Content Control: The Motion Picture Association of America's Patrolling of Internet Piracy in America, 1996--2008.
Ph.D. dissertation, University of Kansas.
2011.

This historical and political economic investigation aims to illustrate the ways in which the Motion Picture Association of America radically revised their methods of patrolling and fighting film piracy from 1996-2008. Overall, entertainment companies discovered the World Wide Web to be a powerful distribution outlet for cultural works, but were suspicious that the Internet was a Wild West frontier requiring regulation. The entertainment industry's guiding belief in regulation and strong protection were prompted by convictions that once the copyright industries lose control, companies quickly submerge like floundering ships. Guided by fears regarding film piracy, the

MPAA instituted a sophisticated and seemingly impenetrable "trusted system" to secure its cultural products online by crafting relationships and interlinking the technological, legal, institutional, and rhetorical in order to carefully direct consumer activity according to particular agendas. The system created a scenario in which legislators and courts of law consented to play a supportive role with privately organized arrangements professing to serve the public interest, but the arrangements were not designed for those ends. Additionally, as cultural products became digitized consumers experienced a paradigm shift that challenged the concept of property altogether. In the digital world the Internet gives a consumer access to, rather than ownership of, cultural products in cyberspace. The technology granting consumers, on impulse, access to enormous amounts of music and films has been called, among many things, the "celestial jukebox."

Regardless of what the technology is called, behind the eloquent veneer is the case in point of a systematic corrosion of consumer rights that, in the end, results in an unfair exchange between the content producers and consumers. What is the relationship of the MPAA to current piracy practices in America? How will Hollywood's enormous economic investment in content control affect future film distribution, exhibition, and consumer reception? Through historical analysis regarding the MPAA's campaign against film piracy along with interviews from key media industry personnel and the pirate underground, this contemporary illustration depicts how the MPAA secures its content for Internet distribution, and defines and criticizes the legal and technological controls that collide with consumer freedoms. [Author Abstract]

8.) **Cuevas, F.**

Student awareness of institutional policy and its effect on peer to peer file sharing and piracy behavior.

Ed.D. dissertation, The Florida State University. 2010.

Higher education institutions embrace internet technology and online services in all aspects of campus life. The internet plays a significant role in the academic environment and is utilized in various institutional business practices. For college students, the internet is an important tool for conducting academic work but it is also utilized for recreational activities such as file sharing and illegal downloading of copyrighted material. Downloading and file sharing of digitized material has become a major concern for institutional policy makers. Responding to outside pressures, institutions have deployed a variety of policies and practices to curb illegal downloading and file sharing activity. Research, however, has not determined how effective awareness of these policies is in influencing student attitudes, behavioral intentions, and behavior. This study fills this gap by exploring the effects of student awareness of institutional policy on behavioral intentions and behaviors toward online file sharing and digital piracy of copyrighted material. Through an online survey, students were asked about their current attitudes and behaviors regarding digital piracy and file sharing, their awareness of institutional policies, and what effects awareness of policies had on their intentions and behaviors toward file sharing and digital piracy. Frequency summaries, simple crosstabs, and multiple regression analysis were utilized to determine the relationships between the variables. Study results suggest that student awareness of policies generally influenced behavior but student attitudes and their behavioral intentions were better predictors of student file sharing and downloading behavior. Awareness effected student behavior by influencing student attitude and student behavioral intention. Results also suggest that demographics characteristics (gender, ethnicity, academic classification, time spent living on campus) had varying effects on the outcomes. The interaction of gender and awareness was the only demographic characteristic that was significant and had any effect on student downloading and file sharing behavior. Females were more aware of policy than males and they were less likely to engage in downloading and file sharing behavior. Males despite having some awareness of policy continued to participate in downloading and file sharing behavior. [Author Abstract]

9.)   **Danaher, B.**

Essays on the economics of digital media and Internet piracy.

Ph.D. dissertation, University of Pennsylvania. 2010.

The rise of Internet media piracy is often cited as the primary source of falling profits in the media industries, as markets for music, movies, and television have diminished since the turn of the millennium. This had led to niche of studies in economics and business-related fields aimed at quantifying losses to the industries and providing potential solutions. In this dissertation I present three empirical papers that use "quasi-experimental" evidence to answer some of the most heavily debated questions in the media industries. In Chapter 1 I ask whether film box office returns are displaced by online movie piracy, and I find evidence that at least billions of dollars are lost each year in the international box office due to piracy. In Chapter 2 I ask whether digital distribution of media--e.g. selling television episodes by digital download on iTunes--can mitigate piracy without cannibalizing physical sales. I find that when a television network removes its content from the iTunes store, it causes a significant jump in piracy of that content but no increase in physical sales through the Amazon.com, the largest online retailer of tv box sets. I also find evidence of a fixed cost to piracy, suggesting that consumers who turn to piracy be unlikely to return to purchasing legally. Finally, in Chapter 3 I turn to the music industry, asking whether the own price elasticity of legal digital music is affected by desirability of online piracy as a substitute good. I find that songs that people tend to pirate exhibit more elastic demand curves in the legal digital market, and that piracy levels for a song increase when that song is raised in price on the iTunes music store. This suggests that firms are constrained in pricing media due to piracy and that firms should use observable piracy data to differentiate pricing across products. [Author Abstract]

10.)   **Davies, C. D.**

A theoretical relationship between guardianship and techniques of neutralization: A qualitative analysis of digital piracy.

M.A. thesis, West Virginia University. 2012.

This research is a qualitative analysis of digital piracy at the height of Napster in 1999. The findings support the notion that technology has given rise to several new techniques of neutralization. In some cases these techniques are completely new and in others they are 21st century updates to traditional techniques. Furthermore, this research uses forum posts from USENET to determine that guardianship as created by Cohen and Felson's Routine Activities Theory is uniquely connected to neutralization based on two unique guardianship qualities, authority and capacity. [Author Abstract]

11.)   **Filby, M. R.**

Cyber piracy: Can file sharing be regulated without impeding the digital revolution?
Ph.D. dissertation, University of Leicester (United Kingdom). 2013.

This thesis explores regulatory mechanisms of managing the phenomenon of file sharing in the online environment without impeding key aspects of digital innovation, utilising a modified version of Lessig's modalities of regulation to demonstrate significant asymmetries in various regulatory approaches. After laying the foundational legal context, the boundaries of future reform are identified as being limited by extra-jurisdictional considerations, and the regulatory direction of legal strategies to which these are related are linked with reliance on design-based regulation. The analysis of the plasticity of this regulatory form reveals fundamental vulnerabilities to the synthesis of hierarchical and architectural constraint, that illustrate the challenges faced by the regulator to date by countervailing forces. Examination of market-based influences suggests that the theoretical justification for the legal regulatory approach is not consistent with academic or policy research analysis, but the extant effect could impede openness and generational waves of innovation. A two-pronged investigation of entertainment industry-based market models indicates that the impact of file sharing could be mitigated through adaptation of the traditional model, or that informational decommodification could be harnessed through a suggested alternative model that embraces the flow of free copies. The latter model demonstrates how the interrelationships between extant network effects and sub-model externalities can be stimulated to maximise capture of revenue without recourse to disruption. The challenges of regulating community-based norms are further highlighted where the analysis submits that the prevalence of countervailing forces or push-back from the regulated act as an anti-constraint to hierarchical and design-based regulation, due to an asymmetry between legal, architectural and traditional market-based approaches, and effective control of the file sharing community. This thesis argues that file sharing can be regulated most efficaciously by addressing this asymmetry through alternative market-based strategies. This can be influenced through extending hierarchical regulation to offer alternative legal and norm-based models that complement, rather than disrupt, the community-based norms of file sharing. [Author Abstract]

12.)   **Forman, A. E.**

An exploratory study on the factors associated with ethical intention of digital piracy.

Ph.D. dissertation, Nova Southeastern University. 2009.

Each year billions of dollars are lost due to illegal downloading and copying of intellectual property. Individuals often perceive little or no consequences as a result of digital piracy. Research has shown that perceived consequences could be used to alter an individual's ethical intention to engage in digital piracy (INT). In addition subjective norm (SUN) may also contribute to INT. Therefore, the goal of this study was to determine the factors of perceived consequences and to assess their contribution, as well as the contribution of SUN, to INT. This predictive study developed a quantitative instrument to measure the contribution of the factors of perceived consequences and SUN on INT. In phase one of this study, an anonymous exploratory questionnaire was used to gather a list of perceived consequences. That list was combined with a list of perceived consequences found through an extensive review of the literature and a survey instrument was developed and used in phase two. After data cleaning, a total of 407 responses remained. Exploratory factor analysis incorporating principal component analysis (PCA) identified eight factors of INT: Personal Emotional Consequences (PEC), Freedom Consequences (FRC), Minor Consequences (MIC), Personal Freedom Consequences (PFC), Personal Moral Consequences (PMC), Network Access Consequences (NAC), Self Worth Consequences (SWC), and Industry Financial Consequences (IFC). A model was developed using Ordinal Logistic Regression to determine the contribution of the eight factors of perceived consequences and SUN on INT. PEC, PMC, and IFC as well as SUN were found to be significant contributors to INT. The Mann-Whitney U test determined that INT was the only factor that showed a significant difference for males. Additionally, gender was a significant contributor to FRC, MIC, PFC, PMC, SWC, and IFC. Each of these factors was more significant for females than males. The Kruskal-Wallis test determined that there were no significant differences in the factors of perceived consequences, SUN, and INT based on age or computer usage. Important contributions of this study include the identification of eight perceived consequence factors not previously known as well as the development of a unified predictive model, addressing all forms of digital piracy. [Author Abstract]

13.)   **Friedman, B.**

Social judgments and technological innovation: Adolescents' conceptions of computer piracy and privacy.

Ph.D. dissertation, University of California, Berkeley. 1988.

This study aimed to provide a characterization of adolescents' social judgments about property and privacy, particularly in relation to innovations that have occurred through computer technology. Sixty-four eleventh and twelfth grade students were interviewed, half on property and half on privacy. The property interview entailed five situations: three involved computer property (copying purchased commercial software to use personally, to give, and to sell), one prototypic property (taking a bicycle), and one potentially ambiguous non-computer intellectual property (taping a purchased record album to give to another). The privacy interview also entailed five situations: three involved computer privacy (accessing another's computer file and not reading the information, reading the information, and changing the information), one prototypic privacy (reading another's diary), and one potentially ambiguous non-computer privacy (reading a letter lying open on someone's desk). Property results showed that copying commercial software in all three situations was often accepted by students who otherwise negatively evaluated the prototypic property violation. This major difference could often be attributed to differing understandings of software as private property and assessments of the consequences of copying software for others. The privacy results showed that most students judged as wrong computer and prototypic privacy acts, and provided welfare, rights, and fairness reasons for their evaluations. Thus, unlike for property, the privacy results suggested that students have largely assimilated electronic information to their existing conceptions of prototypic private information. The one exception was for the situation of accessing another's computer file without reading the information (computer hacking); some students perceived neither harmful consequences nor injustice, and, as such, judged the act as permissible. For both property and privacy rights, students' understandings were often characterized as comprising an overarching moral component that for particular instantiations of the rights could be informed by convention. These results are discussed as they bear on a domain-specific theory of social cognition and on the issue of social judgments in the context of a culture's adaptation to technological innovation. [Author Abstract]

14.)   **Haddad, M. L.**

The war on digital piracy: An analysis of the Stop Online Piracy Act.

M.S. thesis, Drexel University. 2014.

Digital piracy is a widespread and major issue that is estimated to cost media companies such as television networks, movie studios, and recording companies billions of dollars. Throughout the years the United States government has taken various steps to combat piracy. As technology continues to shift and piracy becomes easier and widespread it becomes increasingly difficult to thwart pirates and find solutions that both effectively stopped copyright infringers and protected the liberty of Americans using the internet. The newest attempt to thwart online piracy, House of Representatives Bill 3261, known as the Stop Online Piracy Act (SOPA), was noble in intention but dangerous in proposed execution, and if it had passed the online liberty and freedoms of all Internet users would have been in serious jeopardy. [Author Abstract]

15.)   **Harman, M. T.**

(Didigital) sharing is (analog) caring: An ethnographic study of ideological motivations of digital piracy.

M. A. thesis, University of Georgia. 2012.

In an effort to ascertain the ideological underpinnings of digital piracy, this study intends to display the development of a viable information gift economy within online piracy communities. Conducting a virtual ethnography of members of a private "warez" community, the author proposes identifying anti-capitalist motivations contained in the ideologies of community members. Central to these tendencies is the cooperation and interaction between these individual members of the community, which signifies the emergence of a unique culture that is quickly becoming normalized within the digital sphere. Discussions of repercussions of distributing American content lead to the potential of a form of cultural imperialism, this one mediated through digital technologies. [Author Abstract]

16.) **Hashim, M. J.**

Nudging the digital pirate: Piracy and the conversion of pirates to paying customers.

Ph.D. dissertation, Purdue University. 2011.

Digital piracy is a significant source of concern facing software developers, music labels, and movie production companies. The current legal and technological strategies for mitigating the piracy problem have been largely unsuccessful, as firms continue to invest in litigation and digital rights management technologies to thwart piracy. Their efforts are quickly defeated by hackers and pirates, motivating the behavioral approach taken in this dissertation. In Chapter 2, we consider the common argument from digital media producers and government entities that there are victims of piracy, whereas pirates may perceive their actions to be victimless. Because of the victimless view, in certain circumstances, perceived moral obligations may become important determinants of piracy behavior. In particular, we theorize that attitudes and social norms could influence perceptions of moral obligation as a consequence of the desire to rationalize unethical behavior. We also identify circumstances under which exogenous nudging from a software company can influence the impact of perceived moral obligations on intentions to pirate. Initial purchase and piracy conversion settings are compared to document when the salient constructs become relevant to the potential pirate. In Chapter 3, we explore the role of information targeting and its effect on coordination in a multi-threshold public goods game. We consider four treatments, three in which we give feedback about other member's contributions to a subsample of group members, and another treatment in which feedback is not provided at all. Our three information treatments vary in whom receives the information, which can be given randomly, to those whose contributions are below the average of their group, or to those whose contributions are above the average of their group. Results show improvements in coordination when information targeting is used, leading to an increased contribution to the public good. In contrast, providing information randomly does not improve coordination. Moreover, our random information treatment approximates strategies currently used in practice for educating consumers about business problems such as digital piracy. Thus, our findings provide insights that may be used in practice to enhance education and marketing strategies for reducing the digital piracy problem. The implications of this research may also be employed by management in other contexts where positively or negatively affecting coordination between consumers is of interest. Consumers receive advice from various sources before making consumption decisions. In Chapter 4, we conduct a laboratory experiment using parents and teenagers as the subject pool, bringing a sample of potential pirates and their parents to the experimental laboratory. Experimental treatments are differentiated by the source of the advice regarding the piracy decision, and subjects make their decisions playing our new experimental game--the piracy game. The results are quite intriguing as subjects do respond to advice, albeit in a temporary fashion. Similar to the results described in Chapter 2, increasing moral saliency assists in mitigating piracy, especially when the source of advice is the subject's parent. Overall, this dissertation explores the role of various types of information in impacting purchasing and pirating decisions. We find that pirates may view their actions to be victimless, but this behavior can be mitigated by sending morally-salient information to the pirate. The piracy problem may also be mitigated by carefully targeting information to groups of consumers, rather than taking a blanket approach to informing the population of the piracy problem. Lastly, pirates are receptive to advice about their behavior from sources with whom they have a greater social tie, suggesting the need to carefully consider information delivery channels. [Author Abstract]

17.)   **High, M.**

Piratical designations: Power and possibility in representations of piracy.

Ph.D. dissertation, State University of New York at Stony Brook. 2014.

This dissertation analyzes how designations and representations of piracy define, police, and challenge legitimate production and circulation. From antiquity through the present, the labeling of others as pirates has excluded the less powerful from the authorized distribution of tangible and intangible property. Such discursive exclusion not only defines piracy but also creates it, distinguishing it from other, sanctioned forms of appropriation. This exclusion generates political, legal, and cultural subjectivity, thereby allowing so-called pirates to affect the very discourses and processes from which they are excluded. The first chapter traces the term piracy from its linguistic origin in Ancient Greece to its extension to literary property in 17th century and its current use as a rhetorical weapon in the global information society. Isolating five necessary conditions, this chapter reads piracy across its maritime, intellectual, and digital manifestations, elucidating the success and failure of designations of piracy. The second chapter focuses on the destabilization of these conditions in Hollywood's representations of Caribbean piracy. Due to gaps in the historical record, historians have conflictingly interpreted Golden Age (1650-1720) pirates as criminals, rebels, and anarcho-libertarians. Following these interpretations, but adapting them to its own institutional and hegemonic needs, Hollywood has developed three types of pirates: an actively piratical villain, a reluctantly piratical hero, and a gender shifting temporary pirate. The third chapter develops a genealogy of the anti-piracy media and educational campaigns of the film and recording industries, locating in the

1980's "Home Taping is Killing Music" campaign the appeals that have dominated later campaigns. Recreating the reception of the campaigns of the early 2000's, this chapter combines humanities scholarship on copyright industry rhetoric with social science research on the efficacy of the campaigns to understand why these campaigns have failed to affect the copying norms and practices of millennials. The final chapter analyzes the history and interventions of the groups leading the Swedish Pirate Movement, examining how the *Piratbyrån*, *The Pirate Bay*, the *Missionerande Kopimistsamfundet*, and the *Piratpartiet* humorously appropriate the labels and rhetoric of copyright industry representatives to define themselves and challenge anti-piracy campaigns and legislation. [Author Abstract]

18.)   **Hinduja, S. K.**

Broadband connectivity and software piracy in a university setting.

M.S. thesis, Michigan State University. 2000.

Software piracy has become a significant problem for businesses and educational institutions, and as computer crime continues to proliferate in our information age, its causes and roots merit academic inquiry. This paper attempts to determine whether, and to what degree, high-speed Internet access in a university residential setting facilitates the transferring and distribution of unauthorized software packages. Additionally, it seeks to apply neutralization theory to software piracy to obtain a greater understanding of the factors that influence the commission of this high-tech crime. The study utilized a survey instrument in its methodology, which gleaned valuable information on the motives, rationalizations, and behaviors of software pirates. Independent Samples T-Tests, ANOVA, Correlations, Two-Way ANOVA, and Ordinary Least Squares Regression were utilized to empirically evaluate relationships between variables. A significant relationship was found in that high-speed access is positively related to increased online piracy. Past experience with traditional piracy through the creation and duplication of programs on CDROMs was also found to be a significant predictor of Internet pirating. Finally, neutralization theory was found to be an applicable framework in which to view the deviance. The results of the study are used to suggest policy aimed at combating the onset and perpetuation of unethical and illegal computing activity among students. [Author Abstract]

19.)   **Jankowski, C.**

Music piracy and its criminalization: Understanding the Napster era (1999) to present through Donald Black's theory of moral time.

M.S. thesis, Eastern Kentucky University. 2013.

In the year 1999 Napster, a provider of music downloading software, broke news headlines around the world when copyright infringement lawsuits were filed against the company. Ever since then internet music piracy has been a very controversial topic and a target for criminalization efforts. In the field of criminology there have been few attempts to apply theory to the topic of internet music piracy. Theorization of internet music piracy has mainly focused on the illegal behavior of music piracy, explaining the motivations and knowledge behind it. Something that has been neglected in theoretical work of online music piracy is its criminalization. This thesis topic is significant in that it is a theoretical application test of Donald Black's newest theory, Moral Time. Black, a sociologist from the University of Virginia, who is well known for his works The Behavior of Law and Sociological Justice introduced this new theory in 2011. The Moral Time theory is a theory of why conflicts occur and why some conflicts are worse than others. Using this theory, four key stages of criminalization efforts taken by the music industry are examined and elaborated upon as a means to identify why the music industry chose to take the actions it did against online music piracy. [Author Abstract]

20.)   **Jeong, B.**

Digital piracy: An assessment of consumer piracy risk and optimal supply chain coordination strategies.
Ph.D. dissertation, The University of North Carolina at Charlotte. 2010.

Digital piracy and the emergence of new distribution channels have changed the dynamics of supply chain coordination and created many interesting problems. There has been increased attention to understanding the phenomenon of consumer piracy behavior and its impact on supply chain profitability. The purpose of this dissertation is to better understand the impact of digital piracy on online music channel and optimal supply chain strategies which achieve high levels of coordination. A multi-method approach including survey, mathematical modeling, and simulation are used to (a) analyze the impact of piracy on digital music channel coordination under different contract arrangements, (b) develop theoretical and operational basis for conceptualizing a measurement model of consumer piracy risk, (c) examine the effectiveness of piracy control strategies used to dissuade consumers from illegal music downloads. Findings from this dissertation contribute to the literature on digital piracy, consumer piracy behavior, online channel distribution, and supply chain coordination, and provide several important managerial implications. [Author Abstract]

21.)   **Jinkerson, J.**

*Does music piracy influence purchase
intention?: Adapting Ajzen's Theory of
Planned Behavior model.*
M.S. thesis, Mississippi State University.
2008.

The Recording Industry Association of
America claims to lose millions of dollars
each year from music piracy (RIAA, 2007).
However, instead of causing loss, digital
music piracy may activate norms of
reciprocity in music pirates. When pirating
music, people may feel some obligation to
reciprocate by purchasing music or related
merchandise. The theory of planned
behavior was used to investigate such a
possibility and to provide a framework for
scale development. Reliable scales were
developed for all measured constructs.
Regarding piracy, the RIAA's claim may
have some merit. Specifically, previous
piracy was associated with decreased

reported likelihood to purchase music. However, previous piracy was associated with increased intent to make future music-related purchases. Reciprocity partially mediated this relationship. [Author Abstract]

22.)   **Karakaya, M.**

Analysis of the key reasons behind the pirated software usage of Turkish Internet users: Application of Routine Activities Theory.

Ph.D. dissertation, University of Baltimore. 2010.

The basic reason for protection of intellectual property rights is the necessity to encourage and support innovation and to promote the creation of knowledge. Intellectual property has a functional effect on the creation, development and innovation of the intellectual products which improve our life. Software piracy is one of the important parts of the digital piracy problem, and according to Swinward et al. (1990), software was also the first copyrighted product that was duplicated on a large scale. BSA defined software piracy as the illegal copying, downloading, sharing, selling or installing of copyrighted software. It is difficult to measure accurately the worldwide magnitude of the software piracy problem. According to the Business Software Alliance (BSA) Global Software Piracy Report, the rate of software piracy in 2009 was 43%. This is a serious problem for the world economy, but the problem is more serious in Turkey. According to the BSA 2009 Global Software Piracy Report, the software piracy rate in Turkey was 63% in 2009. If the assumption is made that every instance of pirated software usage equals an amount of loss in the economy, then the impact of the loss on the Turkish economy was 415 million dollars. Before advanced technology and high speed Internet, software piracy was carried out by copying disks or other types of physical objects, but now almost all types of software piracy occur over the Internet. The aim of this study is to explore the factors that contribute to pirated software usage among Turkish Internet users in order to define the dynamics behind the problem of software piracy from the Internet users' perspective. Definition of the reasons behind an existing problem is a crucial part of the problem solving process. With this study the factors behind the problem of pirated software usage will be empirically analyzed from the users' perspective by applying Routine Activity Theory. According to RAT, three major factors that affect criminal activities include access to suitable targets, motivated offenders and the absence of capable guardians. According to the routine activity approach, crime or the risk of crime increases when a motivated offender identifies or encounters a suitable target in the absence of a capable guardian. The concurrent triangulation structure, a mixed method approach, was used in this study. The data collection methods included an online survey questionnaire and online interview forms. The survey questionnaires aimed to measure the targeted Turkish Internet users' attitudes toward pirated software usage as a dependent variable and perceptions about the availability and accessibility of pirated software, motivations behind the usage of pirated software, perceptions about social-legal guardians against pirated software usage as independent variables. Results indicated that motivation, accessibility of pirated software, and perception of social guardians have an impact on Turkish Internet users pirated software usage. The perception of legal guardian had a weak relationship with software piracy attitude. [Author Abstract]

23.)   **Kwan, S. S. K.**

End-user digital piracy: Contingency framework, affective determinants and response distortion.

Ph.D. dissertation, Hong Kong University of Science and Technology (Hong Kong). 2007.

With rapid advances in networking and multimedia technologies, end-user digital piracy has caused more substantial impacts to firms producing digital contents as well as the society at large. In response to the phenomenon, three related research have been conducted. The first research proposes a contingency model to understand the decision making process of end-user digital piracy behavior. The model encompasses two distinct piracy behaviors, namely unauthorized copying and unauthorized sharing, and two distinct digital contents, namely software as well as movie and music. Empirical support of the proposed model is obtained by a large-scale online survey.

While the first research mainly adopts a cognitive perspective, the second research considers affective factors involved in unauthorized sharing that is seldom studied in previous literature. The third research focuses on response distortion that has been troubling many empirical studies on digital piracy. I propose an innovative method for structural equation modeling using data obtained by Randomized Response Technique (RRT) that is often mistaken as only suitable for univariate analysis. The usefulness and feasibility of this new method are supported by large-scale empirical studies on software piracy. [Author Abstract]

24.)   **Leung, T. C.**

Essays on the economics of intellectual property.

Ph.D. dissertation, University of Minnesota. 2009.

This dissertation evaluates the effectiveness of different polices on intellectual property when piracy is growing. The first chapter deals with music piracy. Two beliefs about music piracy prevail in the music industry. First, music piracy hurts music record sales. Second, the only copyright regime that can help the music industry is one that will eradicate music piracy. This chapter finds that the first belief is right while the second is wrong; as the music industry overlooks the complementary effect of music piracy on products such MP3 players. I construct a unique data set from 883 undergraduate students, estimate the demand for music and iPods and show three things. First, music piracy does hurt record sales. Second, music piracy contributes 20% to iPod sales. Finally, I conduct counterfactuals to evaluate the welfare effect of different copyright regimes. While a regime that eradicates music piracy benefits music producers at the expense of students and Apple, another regime in which Apple pays royalties to music producers for legalizing music piracy benefits most students and music producers at the expense of Apple. The second chapter deals with software piracy. Chinese and Hong Kong governments enforce intellectual property rights by eradicating street piracy. This chapter shows that this policy is ineffective due to the emergence of Internet piracy. To support the claim, I construct a unique data set from 222 college students in Hong Kong to demonstrate two things. First, I estimate a random-coefficient discrete choice demand system for Microsoft Office from legal and different illegal sources. Estimates obtained from a Bayesian approach, with a mixture of normal prior, indicates a strong substitution pattern between street and Internet piracy. Second, I conduct counterfactuals in which counterfeit Microsoft Office DVD is not available. Results are threefold. First, only 31% of students who bought counterfeit DVD would choose to buy a legal copy, while approximately 50% of them would switch to download on the Internet. Second, the decrease in consumer surplus ($43/student) outweighs the increase in Microsoft's profit ($6/student). Third, Business Software Alliance (BSA) overestimates the revenue loss due to piracy by up to six times since it ignores the substitution pattern between street and Internet piracy. [Author Abstract]

25.)   **Leurkittikul, S.**

An empirical comparative analysis of software piracy: The United States and Thailand.

D.B.A. dissertation, Mississippi State University. 1994.

Over the last decades, the topic of microcomputer ethics such as software piracy has occupied a great deal of attention from information systems researchers and practitioners. Concerns about software piracy or unauthorized copying of software have been addressed in the management of information systems (MOIS) literature. However, empirical studies, particularly cross-cultural research, on software piracy have been limited. This study provides a cross-cultural study of software piracy by examining software piracy behavior in two different countries: the United States and Thailand. The purposes of this study are to analyze the factors that influence software piracy and to examine the effects of cultural differences on software piracy behavior. In this study, a model for the study of software piracy is developed based on findings in the software piracy literature and the applicable psychological theories including the Theory of Reasoned Action developed by Fishbein and Ajzen (1975) and the Theory of Planned Behavior which was extended from the Theory of Reasoned Action by Ajzen (1985). This study models software piracy as a result of software piracy attitudes, subjective norms, and perceived software piracy control as measured by knowledge, skills, and opportunity. A survey was conducted using 479 students consisted of 229 students at a university in the United States and 250 students at a university in Thailand. Four major hypotheses concerning the difference between Americans and Thais regarding software piracy, attitudes toward software piracy, subjective norms on software piracy, and perceived software piracy control were tested in this study. The significant results of this study show interesting findings that different countries differ in their software piracy behavior, attitudes toward software piracy, subjective norms, and perceived software piracy control. Among the factors affecting software piracy, attitudes toward software piracy were found to have the strongest impacts on software piracy. The findings of this study confirm that environmental and cultural differences have important influences on software piracy behavior. [Author Abstract]

26.)   **Lu, J.**

Software copyright and piracy in China.
Ph.D. dissertation, Texas A&M University.
2009.

This study is to explore how Chinese
software users perceive the issues of
software copyright and piracy. Tianya
Community, the largest online public forum
in China, was selected as a site to study
users' online communication about software
copyright and piracy. Data were collected
over five discussion boards in which software
copyright and piracy were discussed
extensively to retrieve 561 posting threads
with 6,150 messages ranging from March 1,
1999 to June 30, 2007. Lindlof and Taylor's
(2002) qualitative communication research
methods were used to locate and analyze the
recurring dominant themes within the online
discussion by Chinese Internet users. The
study revealed two opposing discourses
existing in software users' perceptions, which

represent globalization and anti-globalization processes surrounding software copyright and piracy. Mittleman and China's (2005) theoretical framework was adopted to interpret material and spiritual tensions between human/material factors, such as software owners, software users, China, and foreign developed countries. Meanwhile, the actor-network theory was applied to map out the roles of non-human/non-material factors, such as new technology, patriotism, and Chinese culture, which function to moderate the existing confrontations between globalization and anti-globalization by preventing software users from totally falling down into either direction of supporting or opposing software piracy. As a result, both forces of conformity and resistance were found to coexist within software users' perceptions and fragment their identities. To deal with fragmented identities, Chinese software users generally adopted a flexible, discriminative position composed by a series of distinctions, between offline purchasing of pirated discs and software download, between enterprise users and individual users, between foreign and local software companies, between freeware/open-source software and copyright/pirated software, between software companies and independent software developers, and between conceptual recognition and behavioral practice. Meanwhile, traditional resistance movements of Polanyi's (1957) counter-movements and Gramsci's (1971) counter-hegemony were reduced from collective contestations with openly declared call for resistance to Scott's (1990) notion of infra-politics that was communicated among software users and expressed in their everyday practice of piracy use but not in public and government discourse. [Author Abstract]

27.)   **Mun, S.**

*Culture-related aspects of intellectual
property rights: A cross-cultural analysis of
copyright.*

Ph.D. dissertation, University of Texas at
Austin. 2008.

This study presented a critical
investigation of the mainstream neo-liberal
approach to global intellectual property
rights protection. There is a widespread but
incorrect perception in the contemporary
intellectual property policy regime that
ineffective copyright protection in developing
countries is primarily an institutional problem
deriving from the lack of economic capacity
and jurisprudential systems. Arguing that the
conventional policy regime offers only a
limited account for global copyright
protection, this study aimed to show that
inadequate copyright protection is not only
an institutional but also historically
contingent cultural problem. For the purpose,

the present study conducted two phases of investigation: (1) a cross-national data analysis of software piracy and (2) comparative historical analysis of authorship in England and China. The first study empirically examined the key determinants of software piracy in the contemporary international market. From multivariate statistical analyses of international data, the study attempted to identify significant factors facilitating software piracy. Special attention was paid to identifying the influence of national culture in software piracy when other institutional factors were controlled. The results showed that a combined outcome of multiple factors including national income, institutional capacity for property protection, in-group collectivist cultural practices, and attitudes toward international intellectual property protection explains the software piracy problem. The second study aimed to provide a more in-depth understanding of the historical linkage between copyright and culture. It traced the historical formation of authorship in English and Chinese print culture to examine whether and why there emerged contrasting conceptions of authorship between them. The findings showed that there was a distinctive historical divergence of material, ideological, and institutional contexts of print culture, which led to different authorship conceptions between England and China. This implies that authorship as the fundamental cultural basis of modern copyright law was not a natural and universal phenomenon inevitably arising from the printing press but rather historically and culturally contingent. [Author Abstract]

28.) **Oh, J. H.**

Piracy propagation of information goods: Theory, measurement, and application.
Ph.D. dissertation, University of Southern California. 2011.

Digital technologies have transformed the traditional structure of production and promotion planning for new information goods. Studies, up to now, have examined implications of file sharing technologies on pricing schemes, protection mechanisms, and distribution strategies of digital contents. However, there is little understanding about the characteristics of piracy propagation process brought about by digital distribution technology. By drastically broadening behavioral options of search, consumption and reproduction of contents, IT-enabled tools may have reshaped conventional way of consumers' engaging in new digital technologies and contents adoption decisions. In this dissertation, I seek to further our understanding of the impacts of the emergence of file sharing technology on consumers' behavior in participating in digital piracy and how such changes brought about by new technology have altered the propagation dynamics of digital contents. I explore several questions regarding the dynamics of digital piracy propagation, influences of heterogeneous population segments on piracy propagation process, and the information role of digital piracy to improve business and policy decisions. My first research question characterizes the demand- and supply-side dynamics of piracy propagation and measures the effectiveness of anti-piracy efforts to curb digital piracy. My second question aims to identify different population segments and their inter-segment influences on piracy propagation. In my third research question, I utilize the consumers' preference information in piracy data to improve market forecasting and promotional decisions. While the first research question characterizes the underlying dynamics of piracy propagation process per title at the aggregated level, the second research question identifies the influence of heterogeneous participants' behavior on the propagation process. The study that addresses the third question is an application to utilize the propagation dynamics for the pre-release forecasting purposes. Overall, my research contributes to a better understanding of the economics of digital products, information products diffusion process, and the economics of digital piracy. [Author Abstract]

29.)   **Peace, A. G.**

A predictive model of software piracy: An empirical validation.

Ph.D. dissertation, University of Pittsburgh. 1995.

There is, perhaps, no more visible ethical (and perhaps financial) dilemma in the software industry today than that of software piracy. This paper details the development and empirical validation of a predictive model of software piracy behaviour by computer-using professionals. The model was developed from the results of prior research in software piracy and the reference disciplines of the theory of planned behaviour and expected utility theory. The study utilized two methodologies in the testing of the model: an experiment and a survey questionnaire. Each methodology yielded significant results indicating a correlation between an individual's intent to commit piracy and the following factors: the individual's attitude towards piracy, peer norms, perceived behavioural control, moral obligation, perception of punishment, perception of probability of audit and perception of software cost. A correlation was also found between intent to commit piracy and actual piracy behaviour. The model performed well in predicting an individual's intent to commit piracy and the actual piracy behaviour of the individual. The results have significant implications for organizations and industry groups aiming to reduce piracy behaviour. [Author Abstract]

30.)   **Prasad, A.**

*Essays on product-introduction timing,
pricing, advertising and piracy in
contemporary media.*
Ph.D. dissertation, The University of Texas at
Austin. 1999.

This dissertation contains three essays
that examine issues in the contemporary
media environment. The first essay
investigates product introduction timing with
specific reference to the motion picture
industry. Every movie is released in
theatrical format and later in video format.
The question is to decide how long after the
theatrical release should the video be
released to the market. Although prior
research has answered this question by
concentrating on the need to prevent
excessive cannibalization of theatrical
revenues, it is shown here that this is not a
sufficient condition. In addition to
cannibalization the decision must be based

on customers' expectations failing which movie profits are less than optimal. The second essay considers a situation where a media program such as an internet site or a video-on-demand movie, can be offered in multiple viewing options to viewers. The options are differentiated only by the amount of advertising they contain and their price. It is shown how price discrimination can be achieved using advertising. In formulating the optimal strategy care is taken that the revenues obtained from the viewers and from the advertisers are both considered. The optimal number of options that should be offered and their price and level of advertising are found. The third essay investigates the issue of software piracy. Piracy results in a loss of revenues because potential adopters may decide to pirate rather than buy the software. However it is found that under specific conditions, tolerating some amount of piracy can be beneficial. This is due to the fact that a software diffuses faster in the presence of piracy. The analysis is initially conducted for a monopoly setting and later extended to a competitive and multiple generation setting. In the latter two cases, relatively more piracy should be tolerated than in the monopoly case. [Author Abstract]

31.) **Reiss, J.**

Student digital piracy in the Florida State University System: An exploratory study on its infrastructural effects.

Ed.D. dissertation, University of Central Florida. 2010.

Digital piracy is a problem that may never disappear from society. Through readily available resources such as those found in a university, students will always have access to illegal goods. While piracy is a global phenomenon, an institution's resources combined with the typical college student's lack of funds makes it more lucrative. Students use a number of methods to justify their actions ranging from previewing media to bringing justice to a corrupt company. While trying to understand the mindset of pirates is one route to deal with piracy, corporations attempted to alleviate the situation using added software encoding. These messages are not always effective, and in some cases caused further damage to consumer morale. Furthermore, students such as Joel Tenenbaum, who continued to pirate music despite warnings from his parents and the recording industry, exemplify the type of person that is unfazed by legal threats, leading to a question of ethics. Students may not feel that downloading is stealing despite numerous warnings from the Digital Millennium Copyright Act and other major media organizations. The predominant solution used by universities involves monitoring the students' network connection to detect Peer-to-Peer (P2P) connections or other connections that involve the transferring of copyrighted goods. Unfortunately, the current tools contain flaws that a crafty student may easily circumvent, undermining any attempts a university's IT department may use to deter piracy. This study explored the nature of piracy prevention tools used by IT departments in the Florida State

University System in order to determine their relative effectiveness. The study also looked into the opinions of the Information Security Officer in terms of alternative piracy prevention techniques that do not involve legal action and monitoring. It was found that most institutions do not use a formal piece of software that monitors for infringing data. They also stated that while their current techniques can do its required task, it was not perfected to a point where it could run autonomously. Furthermore, institutions agreed that students lack proper ethics and concern over the matter of copyright, but were not fully convinced that other preventions methods would be effective. The study ultimately considered monitoring techniques a short-term solution and that more research should be put into finding long-term solutions. It also implied that IT departments should be better funded in order to keep up with the technological gap. [Author Abstract]

32.)   **Rice Richard L., J.**

Behavior, opinions, and perceptions of Alabama public school teachers and principals regarding the unauthorized copying and use of microcomputer software. Ph.D. dissertation, University of Alabama. 1991.

The purpose of this study was to ascertain the nature, scope, and extent of unauthorized copying and use of computer software by Alabama public school students, teachers, and principals by examining the behavior, opinions, and perceptions of public school teachers and principals concerning this practice. The subjects used in the study were 427 Alabama public school computer science teachers teaching grades 9, 10, 11, or 12; 489 non-computer science teachers teaching grades 9, 10, 11, or 12; and 433 principals employed in schools housing grades 9, 10, 11, or 12. A survey instrument was developed to collect data necessary for the study, and this survey instrument was mailed to all subjects. The survey instrument consisted of five sections: opinions about unauthorized copying and use of computer software by educators and students, perceptions about unauthorized copying and use of computer software by educators and students, past behavior of respondents to the survey regarding unauthorized copying and use of computer software, probable future behavior of respondents to the survey regarding unauthorized copying and use of computer software, and a general information section. The general information section collected data regarding professional groups (computer science teachers, non-computer science teachers, and principals), computer use, knowledge of computer software copyright laws, computer availability for teachers and students, and the existence of computer software copyright policies in schools or school districts. Data were examined using one-way analysis of variance, two-way factorial analysis of variance, the Tukey Method of Multiple Comparisons, and chi-square. Frequencies and percentages also were examined for all items on the survey instrument. Results indicated statistically significant differences in opinion in the area of knowledge of computer software copyright laws, and differences in perception in the areas of professional groups and computer use. A statistically significant relationship was indicated between past behavior of the respondents and membership in a professional group. Statistically significant relationships also were indicated between probable future behavior of the respondents and membership in a professional group, and probable future behavior of the respondents and whether or not the respondent used a computer. [Author Abstract]

33.) **Schwender, D. D.**
Reducing unauthorized digital downloading of music by obtaining voluntary compliance with copyright law through the removal of corporate power in the recording industry.
LL.M. dissertation, George Washington University. 2011.

Social norms are the predominant influence on one's behavior and can support or supplant a law. The social norm of digital music file-sharing has effectively prevailed over copyright law, market alternatives, and architectural barriers. An explanation, and possibly an answer, to the issue can be found using a psychological jurisprudence approach to social norms, i.e., a voluntary compliance theory of behavior control. Generally, the standard theory of deterring unwanted behavior through fear of punishment has little actual effect on people's behavior. The two key elements to obtaining voluntary compliance with a law are morality and legitimacy. First, people must perceive the law as consistent with their sense of morality. Second, the public must perceive the making of the law as fair and that the law is fairly enforced by a trusted authority. The main perceived justification for copyright law is to reward artists, i.e., musicians, for their creative works. But, the public perceives the recording industry as the only beneficiary of recorded music purchases. Thus, the current legal structure fails to meet its justification and, in turn, does not comport with people's morals. For similar reasons, people do not perceive the current legal structure as legitimate. The current copyright structure was largely created under massive lobbying pressure from the recording industry for its own benefit. Moreover, the current enforcing authority for the majority of copyright protected sound recordings is the corporate recording industry. People distrust the recording industry due to the knowledge of artist mistreatment and overpriced record albums. Additionally, the highly publicized lawsuits against individual file-sharers appeared unfair to many people, especially considering the previous attempts by the recording industry to limit the transferability of digital music. A possible solution to this non-compliance with copyright law, therefore, could be to return copyright ownership to musicians. This would introduce an external motivating factor that appeals to the morals of digital music file-sharers. At the same time, enforcement of sound recording copyrights by musicians, rather than the large corporate music industry, would legitimate the enforcing authority in the view of file-sharers. Amending the laws to achieve these results could be done by one, or a combination, of the following: (1)

return copyright ownership to recording artists by making the copyright in a sound recording non-transferable or reducing the time frame for which an author may terminate a grant, license, or transfer of a copyright protected work; and (2) codify a time and album limit on recording company contracts with recording artists. [Author Abstract]

34.) **Shemroske, K.**

The ethical use of IT: A study of two models for explaining online file sharing behavior. Ph.D. dissertation, University of Houston. 2011.

The use of peer to peer (P2P) technology to download copyrighted digital material has grown substantially since its introduction to the masses with Napster in 1999. In spite of continued prosecution and law suits costing individuals totals in the millions of dollars, rather than diminish, illegal downloading behaviors continue to grow in popularity raising a question concerning the ethical use of information technology. Why do individuals participate in online file sharing activities in spite of its moral implications? This study investigates the use of two supported models of behavior (Hunt-Vitell General Theory of Ethics, Theory of Planned

Behavior) to explain individuals downloading illegal media files. Specifically, the context used in this study is the downloading of illegal music. Given its nature, this context focuses on the ethical component of the use of technology. While the Theory of Planned Behavior (TPB) has been used to address ethical behaviors, the Hunt-Vitell (HV) model specifically addresses the moral component where it is only implied in the TPB. The two models are compared and contrasted as explanatory tools for illegal downloading behavior and subsequently, the ethical use of IT. A synthesized model based on

components of the two is proposed and tested with significant results. The results of this study are beneficial to organizations attempting to deal with piracy in their retail business models, academic research in terms of validating current models and presenting a new model for investigating ethical use of IT, and extends to educational curricula and even the home regarding a need for expanding the focus of moral development to include an ever growing use of IT in the personal lives of young people. [Author Abstract]

35.)   **Simmons, L. C.**

Cross-cultural determinants of software piracy.

Ph.D. dissertation, The University of Texas at Arlington. 1999.

The software industry has shown phenomenal growth over the past twenty-five years with sales over $20 billion yearly and rising. Piracy has become a major concern with piracy rates in some countries over 90% of total software in use. This study examines five determinants of piracy and their levels in seven countries. Western countries studied include Australia and the U.S. Asian countries studied are China, Hong Kong and Singapore. Two Hispanic countries were included, Colombia and Mexico. Two separate studies are presented. The first is a macro-level study with fifty-eight countries. The explanatory variables include; Individualism/Collectivism, Power Distance, Per Capita GDP and Trade Dependency on the U.S.A regression model is presented. The primary data study includes data from 1,052 people in the seven countries and the explanatory variables include; Power Distance Within a Country, Power Distance Among Countries, Perception of Others Copying and Perceived Wealth to explain Propensity to Pirate. [Author Abstract]

36.)   **Smallridge, J. L.**

Social learning and digital piracy: Do online peers matter?

Ph.D. dissertation, Indiana University of Pennsylvania. 2012.

This study examined the relationship between digital piracy and social learning theory. To the knowledge of this researcher, only one study had tested a full model of social learning theory in relation to digital piracy (Skinner and Fream, 1997). The current study expanded on past work by testing all four components of social learning theory (differential association, differential reinforcement, imitation, definitions). In addition, to being a full test of the theory this dissertation made many additional contributions to the literature; including the creation of new neutralization techniques (DRM defiance, and claim of future patronage), and the examination of the influence of online sources of social learning on digital piracy. Very few studies have examined online social learning in the past (Holt and Copes, 2010, Hinduja and Ingram, 2009). Data for the study was collected through the use of an online survey. The survey was administered via email to a random sample of college students at two eastern universities. The results from this study suggested that offline sources of differential association have a stronger influence on digital piracy than online sources. However, online sources of differential association were also important predictors of digital piracy in multiple models. Other important predictors of digital piracy included positive reinforcement and various neutralization techniques, including one of the new neutralization techniques created for this study. [Author Abstract]

37.) **So, S. S.**

Computer ethics: Youth attitude and behavior in digital piracy.

Ph.D. dissertation, University of Hong Kong. 2010.

As the title of this research is computer ethics: Youth attitude and behavior in digital piracy: a quantitative research based on the data extracted from a data set of a study on the Influence of Information Technology on Hong Kong Youths carried out by the researchers of the Centre of Information Technology in School and Teacher Education (CITE) of the Faculty of Education, The University of Hong Kong was contacted to investigate youth attitude and behavior in digital piracy with a focus on software piracy and the downloading of MP3's or graphics. Exploration on the relationship of demographic factors (such as age, gender, education level) and computer usage pattern with youth attitude and behavior in digital piracy was carried out in the present study. Also, the composite model of attitude-behavior relation found from the literature was modified with the integration of Kohlberg stages of moral development to form the base of the theoretical framework in this research. The research findings were analyzed to reflect the real situation of digital piracy in our society and then give recommendations to schools on the implementation of new IT-related ethical subjects. Finally, limitations and implications of this research were presented to give footprints for future research [Author Abstract]

38.)   **Stanley, H. L.**

From the right or the left: Generation Y and their views on piracy, copyright, and file sharing.

M.A. thesis, University of South Alabama. 2011.

Copyright infringement is not a recent phenomenon; however, the prevalence of the Internet and piracy software has made infringement easier to commit and harder to prosecute. Research identifies the offenders to be in their late-teens and early 20s, an age group that has been christened Generation Y or Millennials. This study confirmed that 19- to 25-year-old college students pirate music at an alarming rate; however, their responses indicate that they are pirating less than previously suggested. This study also determined through survey and focus group research that a disparity exists between legal and cultural mores. According to Posner's theory means-end rationality, if current deterrents fail to prevent future infringements, the justice system must adapt modifications to penalties or jurisprudence is not fulfilling its purpose. [Author Abstract]

39.)   **Sutko, D. M.**

The Production of Piracy from Sea to Sovereign.

Ph.D. dissertation, North Carolina State University. 2013.

This dissertation provides a coherent, interdisciplinary framework for understanding piracy in general and digital piracy in particular. I show that media and sea piracy share a common heritage and I argue it is only by conceptualizing sea and media piracy together that we can understand each better. Through media histories, I contextualize the "digital" and "new" of our contemporary media. Through sea piracy, I reinvigorate the stale and rehashed economic and legal analyses of media piracy. By using sea piracy to denaturalize assumptions about media piracy, I develop a conceptual framework that recasts media piracy as a matter of technological governance rather than symbolic circulation. Technological governance refers to technology both as object of and mode for government. My analysis of piracy resituates contemporary discussions about digital piracy, Internet governance, and technological politics and contributes to critical information studies, digital media studies, communication history, mobilities studies, and piracy studies. The dissertation is organized by problematics rather than periodizations to draw parallels across multiple communication technologies--boats, books, broadcast, broadband--not usually theorized together because of their historical separation. The problematics--emulation, licensing, containers, ports, and reprisal--are historically consistent technologies for discovering, combating, and incorporating pirate practices. I show how these technologies form an anti-piracy apparatus that connects the production of piracy as a problem with the capture of piracy's radical, productive, and always excessive potential. Altogether, I diagram a circuit of intimate yet contested connections among technology innovators, government policy, jurisprudence, content creators, amateurs, experimenters, and more. I show how the manifestations of piracy as a problem, presently and historically, also animate tensions between private/public, control/freedom, amateur/expert, and access/division that are important issues for digital media studies. I conclude that uneasy settlements among powerful stakeholders constrain our possibilities for elaborating a technological politics attuned to living with as little digital and analog domination as possible. [Author Abstract]

40.)   **Tang, P. C.**

Software piracy protection: A losing battle?
M.S. thesis, California State University, Long
Beach. 2006.

There was a Chinese saying: "When the law advances by a foot, the criminals will overtake it by ten-fold". That does appear to be our current state of the software protection dilemma. Over the years, thousands have tried to plug this piracy hole. But at the end, someone always manage to break it wide open. What is the real possibility of solving this problem? Are we indeed fighting a losing battle? This paper will explore some of the problems in software piracy, the problems with our current Digital Rights Management (DRM) software protection methodology, and some promising techniques and technologies that might eventually provide some enforceable mechanism to solve this problem. [Author Abstract]

41.)   Turan, M.

Fighting digital piracy: Can secondary markets for digital goods help?

Ph.D. dissertation, City University of New York. 2011.

The Internet and advanced networking technologies have lead to a rise in the number of pirated digital products. The content industry claims that digital piracy costs several billion dollars per year and is the main reason for declined sales of physical media. Despite the new legislations imposed to address copyright infringements and advanced technological security measures, digital piracy keeps on growing and becomes even a greater threat for copyright owners. Besides deterrent and preventive controls, researchers have also underlined the importance of business models used to distribute and price digital products for the issue of digital piracy. It is believed that an innovative business model that employs a price discrimination technique and an efficient distribution method may help decrease piracy of digital goods. This study proposes a dual channel model that utilizes both a primary and a secondary market for the transaction of digital products, which allows consumers to sell the products that they have purchased by using a legal platform. Implementing a secondary market and coordinating it with a primary market for the distribution of digital goods can decrease the level of digital piracy because of mainly two reasons. First, it offers more profitable transactions for consumers, thus results in an increase in the total number of buyers. Second, availability of a secondary market can increase the degree of how consumers perceive the fairness of digital good transactions. This research first investigates the profitability of the dual channel model for consumers and copyright owners, and the level of piracy in the dual channel model with an economic model. The economic model offers a secondary market within a digital goods retail monopoly framework as a practical alternative to leasing for capturing rents. Model results show that the retailer can increase revenue and market coverage relative to primary market-only sales, which implies a reduction in piracy and an improved relationship with content creators at no cost. Revenue and piracy performance of the proposed model in the presence of piracy is also evaluated by incorporating general model of piracy into the economic model. Additionally, this research uses a behavioral intention model to test the anti-piracy performance of the proposed distribution and pricing mechanism, and compares it with a traditional business model with an experimental survey. Results show that consumers tend to pirate less if there is an available secondary market for the transaction of digital goods. This relation between availability of a secondary market for digital goods and intention to pirate is also mediated by perceived equitable relationship and attitude toward piracy. Finally, it is found that in the presence of a secondary market, consumers perceive legal transactions of digital products more fair. [Author Abstract]

42.)   **Tzenova, S. K.**

Essays on the market structure implications of software piracy.

Ph.D. dissertation, The University of Chicago. 2005.

This paper examines both theoretically and empirically the interaction between market concentration and piracy rates in several European software markets. The specific questions that I address are whether piracy affects market entry and exit rates, restricting the number of firms to just a few competitors strong enough to survive illegal competition. A corollary of this question is which types of firms survive. Larger firms can afford to invest more in copyright protection, and therefore will not be severely hurt by piracy. Moreover, they might even benefit from it through positive network externalities. Alternatively, if individual smaller firms are never the main target of piracy, they are in effect sharing the piracy burden. Thus, one might expect they would be impacted less than larger firms. In other words, does piracy induce "survival of the fittest" effect among suppliers, the fittest firms in this context being the largest ones; or does it lead to market restructuring, moving towards a less concentrated market environment. To answer these questions, I have put together a dataset of industry leader market shares, top ten vendors combined share, number of software firms, as well as piracy percentage rates and dollar levels. Using this data, I estimate a Cournot-justified reduced form model of concentration ratios on software piracy and software imports. The results from this estimation indicate that piracy does indeed discourage market entry, while also solidifying the market position of the largest firms. On average, a 1% increase in either the piracy rate or the piracy multiplier leads to 2.33% increase in the industry leader's market share, and 1.78% increase in the ten-firm concentration ratio. This result fades out for the average firm, indicating that below average firms' shares must decrease in response to piracy, i.e. that for the marginal producers software piracy induces a "survival of the fittest" type of effect. [Author Abstract]

43.)   **Vijayakumar, P.**

"Thou shalt not steal": An analysis of the GATT TRIPS copyright provisions and software piracy in India.
LL.M. dissertation, Queen's University (Canada). 2001.

The thesis examines India's response to the General Agreement on Trade and Tariffs ("GATT") Trade Related Intellectual Property Subjects ("TRIPS") agreement with respect to the TRIPS agreement mandated protection of computer software under national copyright laws, and the mandate of effective enforcement mechanisms for these rights in national laws. In doing this, the thesis first reviews the origins of copyright as a European invention. This examination notes that there is no reported evidence of an indigenous copyright law in India in the millennia preceding British colonization, despite the evidence of a rich, historic Indian artistic and literary culture. The thesis then briefly notes the emergence of international arrangements for copyright protection, beginning with various bilateral treaties and culminating in the multilateral Berne Convention of 1886. This too was a European creation. India became a member of the Berne Convention, from 1886, when Britain adhered its colony to the convention. The thesis then surveys the emergence of the GATT TRIPS agreement, noting its origins in US unhappiness with the perceived inadequacies of the Berne Convention. India's vociferous resistance to the inclusion of intellectual property matters within GATT is noted, a resistance that ultimately proved futile. The thesis then examines the history of the introduction and maintenance of copyright law in India. Copyright arrived in India as a colonial imposition, at first exclusively for the purpose of protecting British Works in India. Early 20th century revisions to the imposed copyright law coincidentally opened the copyright system to Indian authors and publishers. On acquiring independence from Britain in 1947 Indian did not repudiate either its membership in Berne or its inherited copyright law. The inherited law stayed in place until 1957 when an Indian-drafted act was introduced, though that act showed the continuing influence of historic and contemporary British precedents. India subsequently amended its copyright act, such that Indian law anticipated and later exceeded the TRIPS agreement requirements with respect to copyright protection for computer software. The thesis then surveys the emergence of a vital computer software production industry in India. The thesis speculates on the relation between the emergence of this industry and India's ready compliance with TRIPS and its introduction of "TRIPS plus" standards of copyright protection for computer software. The conclusion notes that India has relatively strict laws for the prevention of software piracy. The cause of the continued prevalence of such piracy in India is not the lack of adequate laws, but is primarily various socio-economic factors in India that will take time to eradicate. [Author Abstract]

44.)   **Villazon, C. H.**

Software piracy: An empirical study of influencing factors.

D.B.A. dissertation, Nova Southeastern University. 2004.

Previous research studies on information ethics have addressed the issue of misuse of computer technology through the concepts of reasoned action and planned behavior. These studies are based on attitudes toward behavior, subjective norms, and perceived behavioral control. Current evidence from research indicates self-efficacy can be an important factor with the level of commitment and persistence in the attempt to influence human behavior. Since information ethics requires businesses to assess the ethical behavior of their employees and the security of their information systems, the primary focus of this research is to study the effect of self-efficacy on ethical conduct to computer technology. Four ethical issues affect people in the age of information. These include privacy, accuracy, property or information ownership, and accessibility (Mason, 1986). The misuse of computers and its software has brought the attention of researchers to investigate ethical conduct related to computer use. In line with previous research suggestions, this study empirically examines the role demographic variables and computer self-efficacy variables of gender, age, professional orientation, religious commitment, education, stimulus to act factors, social/legal factors, personal gain factors and situational factors that affect ethical conduct as it relates to computing technology. The survey responses were from 242 students attending a community college and a private university in the Southeastern part of the United States. The results indicated that religious commitment, professional orientation, and gender had no significant effect on ethical computer self-efficacy and ethical intention. Students who had not taken/taken part/or taken a computer law/ethics course and or business ethics course did not impart a difference in the mean ethics score. However, the education level, and age were found to have a significant effect on both ethical computer self-efficacy and ethical intention. Furthermore, the stimulus to act factors, and the social/legal factors were positively related to the propensity to pirate software. [Author Abstract]

45.) **Wagner, S. C.**

Software piracy and ethical decision making.
Ph.D. dissertation, State University of New
York at Buffalo. 1998.

As the use of computers and computer
software increases, so does the propensity
for abuse. Software piracy, the illegal
duplication of software, is a major problem
confronting the software industry. According
to a study by the Business Software Alliance
and Software Publishers Association, $11.2
billion were lost to software piracy in 1996
(Concoran, 1997). The study estimated that,
in 1996, more than half (225 million of the
523 million) of new business software
applications used throughout the world were
pirated (Shapley, 1997), an increase of
nearly 20\% from 1995. Recent research on
software piracy has focused on evaluating
intellectual property protection (Koen and
Im, 1997; Malhotra, 1994; Straub and
Collins, 1990); determining software

protection strategies (Conner and Rumelt, 1991; Gopal and Sanders, 1997; Scoma, 1987); studying the economic impact of software piracy (Givon, Mahajan, and Muller, 1995); describing characteristics of software pirates (Sims and Cheng, 1996); and examining individual attitudes toward software piracy (Glass and Wood, 1996; Leurkittikul, 1994; Taylor and Shim, 1993). This research project focuses on an individual's predispositions to ethical behavior in general in an effort to examine whether their propensity to behave ethically in general indicates their likelihood to pirate software. An ethical decision making model based on foundations in moral philosophy, psychology and business ethics is presented and investigated under several general ethical issues and is specifically examined for the issue of software piracy. Survey data was collected from 259 first and second year MBA students, including Executive MBA students. Data was also collected from 188 undergraduate students for confirmatory model testing. Data analysis via structural equation modeling indicated strong support for major portions of the ethical decision making model. Specifically, in evaluating an ethical scenario or situation, an individual's ethical evaluation, judgment and behavioral intention are related to their actual ethical behavior. Additionally, decisions regarding software piracy are related to general ethical behavior and decisions regarding general ethical scenarios are related to software piracy behavior. [Author Abstract]

46.)   **Wells, R.**

An Empirical Assessment of Factors Contributing to Individuals' Propensity to Commit Software Piracy in The Bahamas. Ph.D. dissertation, Nova Southeastern University. 2012.

Researchers have found that software piracy worldwide over the years has significantly contributed to billions of dollars in lost revenue for many software firms. Software developers have found it difficult to create software that is not easily copied, thus, creating a software protection problem. Software piracy remains a global problem despite the significant effort to combat its prevalence. Over the years, significant research has attempted to determine the factors that contribute to individuals' propensity to commit software piracy. Most of the research on software piracy has been limited to larger societies, with recommendations by researchers to extend similar studies to smaller ones. The literature indicating the need for additional research on this topic in different populations and cultures is significant. Given that, the key contributions of this study were to assess empirically factors such as personal moral obligation (PMO), cultural dimensions, ethical computer self-efficacy (ECSE) and the effect it has on individuals' propensity -- in cultures that support it -- to commit software piracy in smaller geographical locations. Therefore, this research empirically assessed the contribution that PMO, Hofstede's cultural dimension of individualism/collectivism (I/C), and ECSE have made on individuals' propensity to commit software piracy. The study extended the current body of knowledge by finding answers to three specific questions. First, this study sought to determine whether the PMO component contributed to individuals' propensity to commit software piracy in The Bahamas. Secondly, this study sought to determine the level of contribution of Hofstede's cultural dimension of I/C to individuals' propensity to commit software piracy in The Bahamas. Finally, this study sought to determine the contribution of ECSE to individuals' propensity to commit software piracy in The Bahamas. A total of 321 usable responses were collected over a one-month period from students from the school of business at a small Bahamian college, to determine their level of PMO, I/C, and ECSE contribution to individuals' propensity to commit software piracy. This represents, approximately, a 64% response rate. The results showed the overall significance of the models of the three factors in predicting individuals' propensity to commit software piracy. Furthermore, the results indicated that PMO and ECSE subscale PMO and ECSE_DB were significant, however, I/C, and ECSE (as a whole) were not. [Author Abstract]

47.)   **Wilson, C., III.**

Protection of rights in intellectual property: How will public policy control copyright piracy in the age of the Internet?

Ph.D. dissertation, George Mason University. 2001.

The purpose of this dissertation is to examine copyright piracy in the age of the Internet. The digital age has brought both benefits and some costs, one of which is an increase in threats to copying of intellectual property in digital form. Policy to protect intellectual property has traditionally relied on national laws tied to international agreements such as the General Agreement on Tariffs and Trade (GATT). Those who advocate stronger policy state that (1) stronger protection will reduce piracy and (2) threats of trade sanctions will induce countries to implement stronger protection policies. However, current policy is based on assumptions that are becoming obsolete. The

Internet now allows individuals to ignore strong copyright policy by copying protected files in the privacy of their homes. Surveys show that different cultures do not consider copying or sharing software to be theft. This dissertation examines three hypotheses; copyright piracy is decreased (1) by stronger protection policy, (2) by a smaller size communications infrastructure, or (3) by the presence of certain cultural characteristics. Findings show that communications infrastructure size varies inversely with piracy. This finding is unexpected, since the Internet is increasingly involved in copyright piracy and a larger national communications infrastructure allows more access to piracy tools. These findings, when compared with emerging issues, indicate that piracy data reported by industry to the US Trade Representative does not contain information about Internet piracy. The conclusion is that piracy is becoming an individual choice, and copyright policy must be informed by individual motivations. Also, countries of the East are shifting to higher-density communications infrastructures, and countries of the West are shifting towards Eastern views for handling of intellectual property. These shifts will likely result in increased future Internet piracy. To reduce piracy, the copyright industry must explore new business models that offer the convenient features that Internet users want. [Author Abstract]

48.) **Wright, C. K.**

Digital piracy: The investigation of music downloading via peer-to-peer connections on the Internet.

Ph.D. dissertation, Regent University. 2005.

This study focused on the combination of music and technology using the diffusion of innovations theory as a platform for discovery. This theory was appropriate because it combines the technological aspects and communicative aspects of how technology is disseminated to others. Quantitative methodology was used and it was discovered there was no significance in face-to-face interaction in a respondent's decision to download music; however there was significance with respondents' interaction on Internet and with the mass media. Additionally, there was strong significance between a person's religious/spiritual involvement and the likelihood for them to download music or for them to think it was morally wrong. [Author Abstract]

49.)   **Zamoon, S.**

Software piracy: Neutralization techniques that circumvent ethical decision-making.

Ph.D. dissertation, University of Minnesota. 2006.

This research examines the arguments used to condone or condemn the unauthorized duplication of software [a.k.a. piracy]. The research focuses on: (1) extending the existing neutralization framework to include counter-neutralization; (2) describing the relationships between neutralization, moral intensity, and counter-neutralization; (3) revealing neutralization and counter-neutralization arguments in the context of software piracy; and (4) revealing the effects of characteristics of information technology---cost, product type (data/software), and intangibility---on the production of neutralization. Three essays describe the set of studies. The first essay expands neutralization theory to include counter-neutralization techniques and theoretically develops the relationships between moral intensity of an issue and the techniques of neutralization and counter-neutralization. The first essay also includes a review of the existing research and places the neutralization, moral intensity, and counter-neutralization relationships in a general ethical decision-making framework. The second essay is a content analysis of 192 articles from the 5 top-circulating U.S. newspapers in the 1989--2005 timeframe. Results of the empirical analysis confirm the use of both neutralization and counter-neutralization techniques in the public discussion about software piracy. The analysis reveals a disjoint in the types of neutralizations and counter-neutralizations used. Furthermore, the analysis reveals a mismatch in worldviews between rationales that support unauthorized duplication of software and those that reject it. The third essay is a factorial-design experimental study of the effects of product type, product cost, and product intangibility on the types of verbalized neutralizations. A content analysis of 20 scenario-guided concurrent verbal protocols reveals that changes in the cost of information technology influence the type of neutralization techniques used to support unauthorized duplication decisions. Social consensus, a measure of the moral intensity of a situation, is shown to vary based upon information technology characteristics. The dissertation connects various streams of literature as it links and expands fields of ethical decision-making and neutralization. The dissertation is unique in its social constructionist approach to software piracy and its application of neutralization theory to a non-violent action. Because the dissertation cites actual justifications for unauthorized duplication, it has implications for academics and practitioners. [Author Abstract]

Locating Dissertations and Theses

A. Purchase

Many of the dissertations and theses listed in this bibliography are available for purchase through UMI Dissertation Express:

http://disexpress.umi.com/dxweb

By Fax:

800-864-0019

By Mail:

789 E. Eisenhower Parkway, P.O. Box 1346, Ann Arbor, Michigan 48106-1346

800-521-3042

B. Interlibrary Loan

Dissertations and theses may also be requested through Interlibrary Loan via your local public, college or university library.

www.ingramcontent.com/pod-product-compliance
Lightning Source LLC
Chambersburg PA
CBHW071205050326
40689CB00011B/2246